P **Coventry City Libraries**
Schools' Library Service

Evans

It started at a spring, high up in the hills.
Up here the stream flows very fast.

Like most rivers, our river flows
into the sea.

That waterfall is only about 30 metres high. The world's highest waterfall is in Venezuela in South America. It is nearly 1,000 metres high!

Let's go further downstream to the
boat. Then we can journey down
the whole river.

The water in rivers and streams always
flows down a valley.

Now the water is flowing much more slowly than it was higher up the valley.

Lots of streams have joined ours.

Our stream is nearly big enough to be a river.

9

Yes, we'll be sleeping in there for the next three or four days.

No, ducks' feathers are covered with
oil to keep the water out. They are quite
dry and warm underneath.

That's an otter. We're lucky to see him.
Otters are quite rare.

12

He lives in a hole in the bank. Otters have webbed feet like frogs. They are very good swimmers.

13

> Here are some people fishing.

Yes, the river is nice and clean here so there are lots of fish to catch.

14

That's a heron. He's the best fisherman of all. He uses his long, sharp beak to catch his dinner.

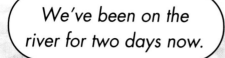

We've been on the river for two days now.

What's that funny old building with the wheel on the side?

That's an old watermill. Years ago that was where corn was ground into flour for making bread.

The river turned the wheel, which turned
the grinding machinery inside the mill.

That's from the town we just passed through. Why don't you collect some with your nets?

I bet the fish and birds don't like it.

No, they don't. They can be hurt by rubbish left in the water. When the water is dirty very few river creatures can live in it.

19

Look everybody, we're coming to a weir.

How will our boat get past it?

Wait and see.

21

Do you see those big gates? They are lock gates. Our boat will go into the lock and be gently lowered as the water is let out. Then we go out the other end.

It's like a staircase in the river.

That's right. Boats can go up a lock as well as down.

Do you see how wide the valley is now?

Look at the cars and lorries going over that big bridge!

It's called a suspension bridge. It hangs from strong steel wires fastened to two tall towers.

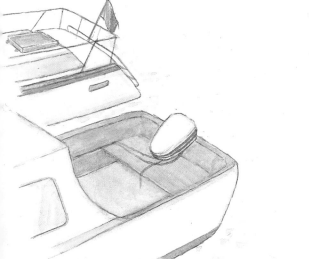

Now we're at the river's mouth.

This is a busy port. Can you see the
fishing boats?

27

These boats are too big to sail up the river, aren't they?

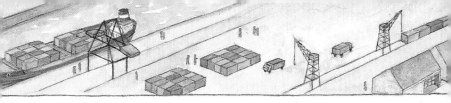

Yes, they unload their cargoes at the quay. Then the cargoes are carried inland by lorries and trains.

I think it's more fun to travel by boat!

Now our river journey is over. How many things can you remember? The answers are at the bottom of the page, but don't peep until you have tried yourself.

1. waterfall, 2. weir, 3. watermill, 4. heron, 5. suspension bridge, 6. lock